My Daily

Name :　　　　　　Date :　　　　　　Day

Schedule

To-do List

- ☐
- ☐
- ☐
- ☐
- ☐
- ☐

Goals for this week

Daily

Notes

My Daily

Name: Date: Day

Schedule	To-do List

Schedule

To-do List

- ☐
- ☐
- ☐
- ☐
- ☐
- ☐

Goals for this week

Daily

Notes

My Daily

Name: Date: Day

Schedule

To-do List

- ☐
- ☐
- ☐
- ☐
- ☐
- ☐

Goals for this week

Daily

Notes

My Daily

Name: Date: Day

Schedule

To-do List

- ☐
- ☐
- ☐
- ☐
- ☐
- ☐

Goals for this week

Daily

_____
_____
_____

Notes

_____
_____
_____

My Daily

Name: _____ Date: _____ Day _____

Schedule

To-do List

- ☐
- ☐
- ☐
- ☐
- ☐
- ☐

Goals for this week

Daily

_____

_____

_____

Notes

_____

_____

_____

My Daily

Name: Date: Day

Schedule

To-do List

- ☐
- ☐
- ☐
- ☐
- ☐
- ☐

Goals for this week

Daily   Notes

_____   _____

_____   _____

_____   _____

My Daily

Name:　　　　　　Date:　　　　　　Day

Schedule

To-do List

- ☐
- ☐
- ☐
- ☐
- ☐
- ☐

Goals for this week

Daily

Notes

My Daily

Name: Date: Day

Schedule

To-do List

- [ ]
- [ ]
- [ ]
- [ ]
- [ ]
- [ ]

Goals for this week

Daily

Notes

My Daily

Name: Date: Day

Schedule

To-do List

- ☐
- ☐
- ☐
- ☐
- ☐
- ☐

Goals for this week

Daily

Notes

My Daily

Name: Date: Day

Schedule

To-do List

- [ ]
- [ ]
- [ ]
- [ ]
- [ ]
- [ ]

Goals for this week

Daily

_____

_____

_____

Notes

_____

_____

_____

My Daily

Name: Date: Day

Schedule	To-do List
	☐
	☐
	☐
	☐
	☐
	☐

Goals for this week

Daily

_____

_____

_____

Notes

_____

_____

_____

My Daily

Name: Date: Day

Schedule

To-do List

- ☐
- ☐
- ☐
- ☐
- ☐
- ☐

Goals for this week

Daily

_____
_____
_____

Notes

_____
_____
_____

My Daily

Name :   Date :   Day

Schedule

To-do List

- ☐
- ☐
- ☐
- ☐
- ☐
- ☐

Goals for this week

Daily

Notes

My Daily

Name: Date: Day

Schedule

To-do List

- ☐
- ☐
- ☐
- ☐
- ☐
- ☐

Goals for this week

Daily

Notes

My Daily

Name: Date: Day

Schedule

To-do List

- ☐
- ☐
- ☐
- ☐
- ☐
- ☐

Goals for this week

Daily

_____

_____

_____

Notes

_____

_____

_____

My Daily

Name: Date: Day

Schedule	To-do List

Schedule

To-do List

- ☐
- ☐
- ☐
- ☐
- ☐
- ☐

Goals for this week

Daily

Notes

My Daily

Name: Date: Day

Schedule

To-do List

- ☐
- ☐
- ☐
- ☐
- ☐
- ☐

Goals for this week

Daily

Notes

My Daily

Name: Date: Day

Schedule

To-do List

- ☐
- ☐
- ☐
- ☐
- ☐
- ☐

Goals for this week

Daily   Notes

My Daily

Name :   Date :   Day

Schedule

To-do List

- ☐
- ☐
- ☐
- ☐
- ☐
- ☐

Goals for this week

Daily   Notes

My Daily

Name: Date: Day

Schedule

To-do List

- [ ]
- [ ]
- [ ]
- [ ]
- [ ]
- [ ]

Goals for this week

Daily

Notes

My Daily

Name: Date: Day

Schedule

To-do List

- ☐
- ☐
- ☐
- ☐
- ☐
- ☐

Goals for this week

Daily

Notes

My Daily

Name: Date: Day

Schedule

To-do List

- ☐
- ☐
- ☐
- ☐
- ☐
- ☐

Goals for this week

Daily

_____
_____
_____

Notes

_____
_____
_____

My Daily

Name: Date: Day

Schedule

To-do List

- ☐
- ☐
- ☐
- ☐
- ☐
- ☐

Goals for this week

Daily

Notes

My Daily

Name: Date: Day

Schedule

To-do List

- ☐
- ☐
- ☐
- ☐
- ☐
- ☐

Goals for this week

Daily

Notes

My Daily

Name :　　　　　　　　　Date :　　　　　　　Day

Schedule

To-do List

- ☐
- ☐
- ☐
- ☐
- ☐
- ☐

Goals for this week

Daily

Notes

My Daily

Name: Date: Day

Schedule

To-do List

- ☐
- ☐
- ☐
- ☐
- ☐
- ☐

Goals for this week

Daily   Notes

My Daily

Name: Date: Day

Schedule

To-do List

- [ ]
- [ ]
- [ ]
- [ ]
- [ ]
- [ ]

Goals for this week

Daily

Notes

My Daily

Name: Date: Day

Schedule	To-do List
	☐
	☐
	☐
	☐
	☐
	☐

Goals for this week

Daily

_____

_____

_____

Notes

_____

_____

_____

My Daily

Name: Date: Day

Schedule

To-do List

- [ ]
- [ ]
- [ ]
- [ ]
- [ ]
- [ ]

Goals for this week

Daily   Notes

My Daily

Name: Date: Day

Schedule

To-do List

- ☐
- ☐
- ☐
- ☐
- ☐
- ☐

Goals for this week

Daily

_____

_____

_____

Notes

_____

_____

_____

My Daily

Name: Date: Day

Schedule	To-do List

To-do List
- [ ]
- [ ]
- [ ]
- [ ]
- [ ]
- [ ]

Goals for this week

Daily

Notes

My Daily

Name: Date: Day

Schedule

To-do List

- ☐
- ☐
- ☐
- ☐
- ☐
- ☐

Goals for this week

Daily

Notes

My Daily

Name: Date: Day

Schedule

To-do List

- [ ]
- [ ]
- [ ]
- [ ]
- [ ]
- [ ]

Goals for this week

Daily   Notes

My Daily

Name: Date: Day

Schedule

To-do List

- [ ]
- [ ]
- [ ]
- [ ]
- [ ]
- [ ]

Goals for this week

Daily

_____
_____
_____

Notes

_____
_____
_____

My Daily

Name: Date: Day

Schedule

To-do List

- ☐
- ☐
- ☐
- ☐
- ☐
- ☐

Goals for this week

Daily

Notes

My Daily

Name: Date: Day

Schedule

To-do List

- [ ]
- [ ]
- [ ]
- [ ]
- [ ]
- [ ]

Goals for this week

Daily   Notes

My Daily

Name :   Date :   Day

Schedule

To-do List

- ☐
- ☐
- ☐
- ☐
- ☐
- ☐

Goals for this week

Daily

Notes

My Daily

Name: Date: Day

Schedule

To-do List

- [ ]
- [ ]
- [ ]
- [ ]
- [ ]
- [ ]

Goals for this week

Daily

Notes

My Daily

Name: Date: Day

Schedule

To-do List

- ☐
- ☐
- ☐
- ☐
- ☐
- ☐

Goals for this week

Daily   Notes

_____   _____
_____   _____
_____   _____

My Daily

Name: _____ Date: _____ Day _____

Schedule

To-do List

- ☐
- ☐
- ☐
- ☐
- ☐
- ☐

Goals for this week

Daily

_____

_____

_____

Notes

_____

_____

_____

My Daily

Name: Date: Day

Schedule

To-do List

☐
☐
☐
☐
☐
☐

Goals for this week

Daily   Notes

My Daily

Name :   Date :   Day

Schedule

To-do List

- ☐
- ☐
- ☐
- ☐
- ☐
- ☐

Goals for this week

Daily

_____
_____
_____

Notes

_____
_____
_____

My Daily

Name: Date: Day

Schedule

To-do List

- [ ]
- [ ]
- [ ]
- [ ]
- [ ]
- [ ]

Goals for this week

Daily

Notes

My Daily

Name: Date: Day

Schedule

To-do List

- ☐
- ☐
- ☐
- ☐
- ☐
- ☐

Goals for this week

Daily

Notes

My Daily

Name: Date: Day

Schedule

To-do List

- [ ]
- [ ]
- [ ]
- [ ]
- [ ]
- [ ]

Goals for this week

Daily

Notes

My Daily

Name: Date: Day

Schedule

To-do List

- [ ]
- [ ]
- [ ]
- [ ]
- [ ]
- [ ]

Goals for this week

Daily

Notes

My Daily

Name: Date: Day

Schedule

To-do List

- [ ]
- [ ]
- [ ]
- [ ]
- [ ]
- [ ]

Goals for this week

Daily   Notes

_____   _____
_____   _____
_____   _____

My Daily

Name: Date: Day

Schedule

To-do List

☐

☐

☐

☐

☐

☐

Goals for this week

Daily

_____

_____

_____

Notes

_____

_____

_____

My Daily

Name：   Date：   Day

Schedule

To-do List

- ☐
- ☐
- ☐
- ☐
- ☐
- ☐

Goals for this week

Daily

Notes

My Daily

Name: Date: Day

Schedule

To-do List

- ☐
- ☐
- ☐
- ☐
- ☐
- ☐

Goals for this week

Daily

Notes

My Daily

Name: _____ Date: _____ Day

Schedule

To-do List

- ☐
- ☐
- ☐
- ☐
- ☐
- ☐

Goals for this week

Daily

_____

_____

_____

Notes

_____

_____

_____

My Daily

Name: Date: Day

Schedule

To-do List

- [ ]
- [ ]
- [ ]
- [ ]
- [ ]
- [ ]

Goals for this week

Daily

Notes

My Daily

Name :   Date :   Day

Schedule

To-do List

- [ ]
- [ ]
- [ ]
- [ ]
- [ ]
- [ ]

Goals for this week

Daily   Notes

_____   _____
_____   _____
_____   _____

My Daily

Name: Date: Day

Schedule	To-do List

To-do List
- ☐
- ☐
- ☐
- ☐
- ☐
- ☐

Goals for this week

Daily

Notes

My Daily

Name: Date: Day

Schedule

To-do List

- ☐
- ☐
- ☐
- ☐
- ☐
- ☐

Goals for this week

Daily

Notes

My Daily

Name: Date: Day

Schedule

To-do List

- ☐
- ☐
- ☐
- ☐
- ☐
- ☐

Goals for this week

Daily

Notes

My Daily

Name: Date: Day

Schedule

To-do List

- [ ]
- [ ]
- [ ]
- [ ]
- [ ]
- [ ]

Goals for this week

Daily

Notes

My Daily

Name: Date: Day

Schedule

To-do List

- ☐
- ☐
- ☐
- ☐
- ☐
- ☐

Goals for this week

Daily   Notes

My Daily

Name :   Date :   Day

Schedule

To-do List

- ☐
- ☐
- ☐
- ☐
- ☐
- ☐

Goals for this week

Daily   Notes

My Daily

Name: Date: Day

Schedule

To-do List

- ☐
- ☐
- ☐
- ☐
- ☐
- ☐

Goals for this week

Daily

_____
_____
_____

Notes

_____
_____
_____

My Daily

Name: Date: Day

Schedule

To-do List

- ☐
- ☐
- ☐
- ☐
- ☐
- ☐

Goals for this week

Daily

Notes

My Daily

Name: Date: Day

Schedule

To-do List

- ☐
- ☐
- ☐
- ☐
- ☐
- ☐

Goals for this week

Daily   Notes

My Daily

Name: Date: Day

Schedule

To-do List

- [ ]
- [ ]
- [ ]
- [ ]
- [ ]
- [ ]

Goals for this week

Daily

Notes

My Daily

Name: Date: Day

Schedule

To-do List

- [ ]
- [ ]
- [ ]
- [ ]
- [ ]
- [ ]

Goals for this week

Daily

Notes

My Daily

Name: Date: Day

Schedule

To-do List

- ☐
- ☐
- ☐
- ☐
- ☐
- ☐

Goals for this week

Daily   Notes

_____   _____
_____   _____
_____   _____

My Daily

Name: Date: Day

Schedule

To-do List

- [ ]
- [ ]
- [ ]
- [ ]
- [ ]
- [ ]

Goals for this week

Daily

Notes

My Daily

Name: _____   Date: _____   Day _____

Schedule	To-do List
	☐
	☐
	☐
	☐
	☐
	☐

Goals for this week

Daily

Notes

My Daily

Name: Date: Day

Schedule

To-do List

- ☐
- ☐
- ☐
- ☐
- ☐
- ☐

Goals for this week

Daily

Notes

My Daily

Name: Date: Day

Schedule

To-do List

- ☐
- ☐
- ☐
- ☐
- ☐
- ☐

Goals for this week

Daily

Notes

My Daily

Name: Date: Day

Schedule

To-do List

- ☐
- ☐
- ☐
- ☐
- ☐
- ☐

Goals for this week

Daily   Notes

_____   _____
_____   _____
_____   _____

My Daily

Name :　　　　　　Date :　　　　　　Day

Schedule

To-do List

- [ ]
- [ ]
- [ ]
- [ ]
- [ ]
- [ ]

Goals for this week

Daily

Notes

My Daily

Schedule	To-do List
	☐
	☐
	☐
	☐
	☐
	☐

Goals for this week

Daily

Notes

My Daily

Name: Date: Day

Schedule

To-do List

- ☐
- ☐
- ☐
- ☐
- ☐
- ☐

Goals for this week

Daily

_____
_____
_____

Notes

_____
_____
_____

My Daily

Name: Date: Day

Schedule

To-do List

- [ ]
- [ ]
- [ ]
- [ ]
- [ ]
- [ ]

Goals for this week

Daily

Notes

My Daily

Name: _____ Date: _____ Day

Schedule

To-do List

- ☐
- ☐
- ☐
- ☐
- ☐
- ☐

Goals for this week

Daily
_____
_____
_____

Notes
_____
_____
_____

My Daily

Name: Date: Day

Schedule

To-do List

- [ ]
- [ ]
- [ ]
- [ ]
- [ ]
- [ ]

Goals for this week

Daily

Notes

My Daily

Name: Date: Day

Schedule	To-do List

To-do List
- ☐
- ☐
- ☐
- ☐
- ☐
- ☐

Goals for this week

Daily

Notes

My Daily

Name: Date: Day

Schedule

To-do List

- [ ]
- [ ]
- [ ]
- [ ]
- [ ]
- [ ]

Goals for this week

Daily

Notes

My Daily

Name: Date: Day

Schedule

To-do List

- [ ]
- [ ]
- [ ]
- [ ]
- [ ]
- [ ]

Goals for this week

Daily   Notes

My Daily

Name: _____ Date: _____ Day _____

Schedule

To-do List

- ☐
- ☐
- ☐
- ☐
- ☐
- ☐

Goals for this week

Daily

_____
_____
_____

Notes

_____
_____
_____

My Daily

Name: Date: Day

Schedule

To-do List

- [ ]
- [ ]
- [ ]
- [ ]
- [ ]
- [ ]

Goals for this week

Daily

Notes

My Daily

Name: Date: Day

Schedule

To-do List

- [ ]
- [ ]
- [ ]
- [ ]
- [ ]
- [ ]

Goals for this week

Daily

Notes

My Daily

Name:　　　　　Date:　　　　　Day

Schedule

To-do List

- ☐
- ☐
- ☐
- ☐
- ☐
- ☐

Goals for this week

Daily

Notes

My Daily

Name: Date: Day

Schedule

To-do List

- ☐
- ☐
- ☐
- ☐
- ☐
- ☐

Goals for this week

Daily

_____
_____
_____

Notes

_____
_____
_____

My Daily

Name :   Date :   Day

Schedule

To-do List

- ☐
- ☐
- ☐
- ☐
- ☐
- ☐

Goals for this week

Daily

Notes

My Daily

Name: _____   Date: _____   Day _____

Schedule

To-do List

- ☐
- ☐
- ☐
- ☐
- ☐
- ☐

Goals for this week

Daily

Notes

My Daily

Name: _____   Date: _____   Day

Schedule

To-do List

☐
☐
☐
☐
☐
☐

Goals for this week

Daily
_____
_____
_____

Notes
_____
_____
_____

My Daily

Name: Date: Day

Schedule

To-do List

- ☐
- ☐
- ☐
- ☐
- ☐
- ☐

Goals for this week

Daily

_____

_____

_____

Notes

_____

_____

_____

My Daily

Name: Date: Day

Schedule

To-do List

- [ ]
- [ ]
- [ ]
- [ ]
- [ ]
- [ ]

Goals for this week

Daily

Notes

My Daily

Name: Date: Day

Schedule

To-do List

- [ ]
- [ ]
- [ ]
- [ ]
- [ ]
- [ ]

Goals for this week

Daily

Notes

My Daily

Name: Date: Day

Schedule

To-do List

- ☐
- ☐
- ☐
- ☐
- ☐
- ☐

Goals for this week

Daily

Notes

My Daily

Name: Date: Day

Schedule

To-do List

- [ ]
- [ ]
- [ ]
- [ ]
- [ ]
- [ ]

Goals for this week

Daily

Notes

My Daily

Name: Date: Day

Schedule

To-do List

- [ ]
- [ ]
- [ ]
- [ ]
- [ ]
- [ ]

Goals for this week

Daily

Notes

My Daily

Name: Date: Day

Schedule

To-do List

- ☐
- ☐
- ☐
- ☐
- ☐
- ☐

Goals for this week

Daily

Notes

My Daily

Name: Date: Day

Schedule

To-do List

- ☐
- ☐
- ☐
- ☐
- ☐
- ☐

Goals for this week

Daily

_____
_____
_____

Notes

_____
_____
_____

My Daily

Name: Date: Day

Schedule

To-do List

- ☐
- ☐
- ☐
- ☐
- ☐
- ☐

Goals for this week

Daily

Notes

My Daily

Name: Date: Day

Schedule

To-do List

- ☐
- ☐
- ☐
- ☐
- ☐
- ☐

Goals for this week

Daily

Notes

My Daily

Name: Date: Day

Schedule

To-do List

- [ ]
- [ ]
- [ ]
- [ ]
- [ ]
- [ ]

Goals for this week

Daily

Notes

My Daily

Name:　　　　　　　Date:　　　　　　　Day

Schedule

To-do List

- ☐
- ☐
- ☐
- ☐
- ☐
- ☐

Goals for this week

Daily

Notes

My Daily

Name: Date: Day

Schedule

To-do List

- [ ]
- [ ]
- [ ]
- [ ]
- [ ]
- [ ]

Goals for this week

Daily

Notes

My Daily

Name: Date: Day

Schedule

To-do List

- ☐
- ☐
- ☐
- ☐
- ☐
- ☐

Goals for this week

Daily   Notes

My Daily

Name: Date: Day

Schedule

To-do List

- ☐
- ☐
- ☐
- ☐
- ☐
- ☐

Goals for this week

Daily

Notes

My Daily

Name :   Date :   Day

Schedule

To-do List

- [ ]
- [ ]
- [ ]
- [ ]
- [ ]
- [ ]

Goals for this week

Daily

Notes

Printed in Great Britain
by Amazon

38029763R00061